Great work Gary! Congratulations on your
1988 membership to EPC and hopefully to many more!

Jack

Dedicated to Pat's Parents,
Everett and Helen Clauson.

ISBN 0-936189-01-0
Library of Congress Catalog No. 85-063526

Printed in Hong Kong by Everbest Printing Co. Ltd.
Published by Petruska–Petruska Publishing
435 Water Street
Excelsior, Minnesota 55331 U.S.A.

When ordering additional copies, write
the publisher.

CARIBBEAN ISLANDS

Photographs by Hans and Pat Petruska
Introduction by Dr. Lars Wilhelmsson

PETRUSKA–PETRUSKA PUBLISHING

Introduction

People are attracted to the Caribbean for its breath-taking beauty, ideal climate, luscious food, delightful shopping, romantic atmosphere, quietness, fun and relaxation. Hans and Pat Petruska have traveled in the Caribbean for ten years and have visited over a dozen islands during the different seasons and testify to its incredible beauty: "The beauty of God is all around us if only we open our eyes and discover it." As Christian artists, Hans and Pat readily discovered God's creation of pristine beauty in the Caribbean.

Tropical islands, the bright sunshine, white and black sand beaches, clear with different shades of aqua blue exemplify the Caribbean. Cows, dogs, goats and other animals roam freely on the islands.

The Caribbean embraces two kinds of islands. *Volcanic* islands are lush, green and mountainous, with curving and steep, winding roads. Here fruit grows wild and rain is plentiful, with the high mountains attracting the clouds. The *coral* islands are flat and dry with cactus growing everywhere.

Between Grenada and St. Vincent, the Grenadines form an island chain of rugged mountain terrace, lush forests, natural beaches along clear waters, all contributing to the dramatic scenery. The beach at Magens Bay, St. Thomas, is considered one of the ten most beautiful beaches in the world. Antigua boasts 365 beaches, one for each day of the year, along its hundreds of secluded bays, small inlets and coral reefs. Along with the beautiful beaches, long-established hotels and impressive apartments make Antigua one of the most popular vacation islands.

Not blessed with beauty alone, ideal climate also prevails in the islands, with gentle trade winds and a year-round average temperature of 80 degrees.

The residents of St. Maarten/St. Martin proudly point out that while on other Caribbean islands, one "eats," but on St. Maarten/St. Martin one "dines." Hans' and Pat's favorite place to dine is Antoine's in St. Maarten/St. Martin.

The island of Guadeloupe, which gives the visitor an immediate sense of cosmopolitan France itself, is also well-known for its gastronomic delights. Food is flown in daily from Paris to ensure freshness at its best.

For variety in eating, St. Thomas is hard to beat. An incredible selection of fine cuisine includes entrees from Mexican to Caribbean, from Oriental to Italian.

San Juan is the hub of the Caribbean where most people come and go. Cruise ships begin their luxurious sailings from San Juan to take their passengers all over the Caribbean. It is the largest of the islands and is made up of countless valleys with its rich green surroundings.

The A,B,C islands–Aruba, Bonaire, Curacao– are coral islands that provide picturesque scenery. Curacao is one of the larger ports with its Dutch flavor and lively atmosphere. Hans' and Pat's favorite restaurant and hotel here is Park Plaza with its sumptuous food and attractive accommodations.

The kind and friendly people of Jamaica make it one of Petruska's special islands to visit. In addition to its "great" people it boasts of many fresh water rivers.

In the Caribbean, a shopper's delight, shops abound where a person can browse and bring home "duty-free" items. The best places for duty-free bargains are probably St. Maarten/St. Martin and St. Thomas in the U.S. Virgin Islands. On both the Dutch and French side of St. Maarten/St. Martin Islands, no local duties or taxes are imposed either. St. Thomas has imports from around the world with prices substantially lower than on the U.S. mainland. Americans are given an extra duty-free allowance. Exquisite jewelry, fine leather goods, expensive perfumes, fine clothing, and up-to-date electronics are found at bargain prices.

Those looking for the prestige label, "Made in France" find that Martinique provides a shopper's paradise. Here, fashionable little boutiques sell Paris couture, Riviera resortwear, beautiful French accessories, French wines, spices and varied exotica. With the dollar being so high it is easy to find low prices on perfumes, jewelry, crystal and china, swimsuits, model dresses, madras-dressed dolls, ceramics, shell figures, products in bamboo, wicker and straw, and brilliantly colored tapestries depicting aspects of Martinique life.

Montserrat is the ideal place to shop for craft items. A glass cutting operation at Dutcher's Studio in Olveston produces hand-painted and most unusual items. Near Plymouth at the Montserrat Tannery is one of only two or three places in the Caribbean where skins are processed to create sandals, belts, and a variety of leather products. Those looking for fine quality shawls, table-mats and other cloth articles will find them at the Montserrat Sea Island Cotton Company where 112 modern looms continually spin out materials for such items.

The home of Caribee Clothes is Charlestown on the island of Nevis where top-quality hand-embroidered clothes are made and exported throughout the Caribbean and overseas. Nevis is also renowned for its attractive hotels known as "The Inns of Nevis," mostly based on converted and restored plantation houses with much of their original stonework still intact.

Martinique boasts a variety of hotels spread throughout the entire island–some large and stylish, others small, intimate and charming. Probably the best known is the Bakoua Beach Hotel at Pointe du Bout, located across the bay from Fort-de-France, near the village of Trois-Ilets. This is next door to the largest of Martinique's hotels, the Meridien, which has 303 tastefully decorated rooms overlooking the bay.

Scuba divers find the Caribbean the perfect environment with its tropical islands, bright sunshine, clear, warm waters and the abundance of marine life. And the windward islands (Dominica, St. Lucia, St. Vincent, the Grenadines and Grenada) cannot be beat when it comes to scuba diving, with an underwater chain of 220 miles inhabited by exotic reel life such as squid, octopus, sergeant majors, flying gurnards, peppermintstick lobsters, high hats and moray eels.

The British Virgin Islands are ideal for sailing. The islands are quiet, uncommercialized and extremely picturesque. Their sheltered waters make these islands attractive to sailors who like beautiful and safe sailing. There is plenty of privacy and solitude with miles of unspoiled beaches and concealed bays. The climate is particularly healthy with extreme heat tempered by the trade winds.

Those who want to get away from crowds and bustle will find Dominica just the right place. This island is volcanic in origin and, though mountainous, is covered in rich tropical foliage. The mountains with their coursing streams flowing down to the sea provide perfect fresh water bathing to be found nowhere else in the Caribbean. Dominica is known for its forests and waterfalls and is rich in tropical fruits and vegetables.

To the busy American, the relaxed atmosphere of the Caribbean will often seem attractive. A typical saying which amused both Hans and Pat is, "no problem." At one restaurant as they received the wrong meal they were told by the waiter, "No problem, you eat it, you'll like it." Life on the island moves at a slow pace.

Such an atmosphere fosters a different perspective on life. There is time to unwind, sit back and meditate. There is time for husbands and wives to think about each other and to express their inner and deeper feelings toward one another. To Hans and Pat this has been extremely helpful in their continuing search for intimacy in their marriage and with their Lord and Savior, Jesus Christ. Their time to think has further deepened their conviction that life must be lived with God in charge, if anything of permanent value is to be accomplished. Time must be seen in relation to eternity. To live only for this life finds no deep satisfaction. It is to be wise for the moment but foolish for eternity.

Hans and Pat recognize that their talents are God-given and that photography is how they express themselves. They put it: "We put people's emotions on paper."

The way by which they can communicate with their artistic talents makes Hans and Pat excited about their profession. The Journal of American Insurance claims that people learn one percent through their sense of taste, one-and-a-half percent through touch, three-and-a-half percent by smelling, eleven percent through hearing and *eighty-three percent through sight*. People retain ten percent of what they read, twenty percent of what they hear, *thirty percent of what they see and fifty percent of what they see and hear.* This makes photography one of the most dynamic forms of communication.

Hans and Pat testify that photography is an art form to which they give one-hundred percent of themselves. They point out, "The directions photography can take you are endless and only limited by how much you give of yourself and the reach of your imagination." Unique photography, according to the Petruskas, requires "imagination, determination and dedication."

"The success of a photograph," according to Hans and Pat, "lies in the eye and in the mind of the photographer." They assert that the photographer "does not find pictures, he creates them." This book is a confirmation of that viewpoint.

As believers in Jesus Christ, Hans and Pat have come to look upon all this breath-taking beauty as something created by Almighty God to show His handiwork and for us to appreciate and enjoy. Our logical response to God's goodness is that we should all use the potential God has given to us to bring glory to Him.

Dr. Lars Wilhelmsson

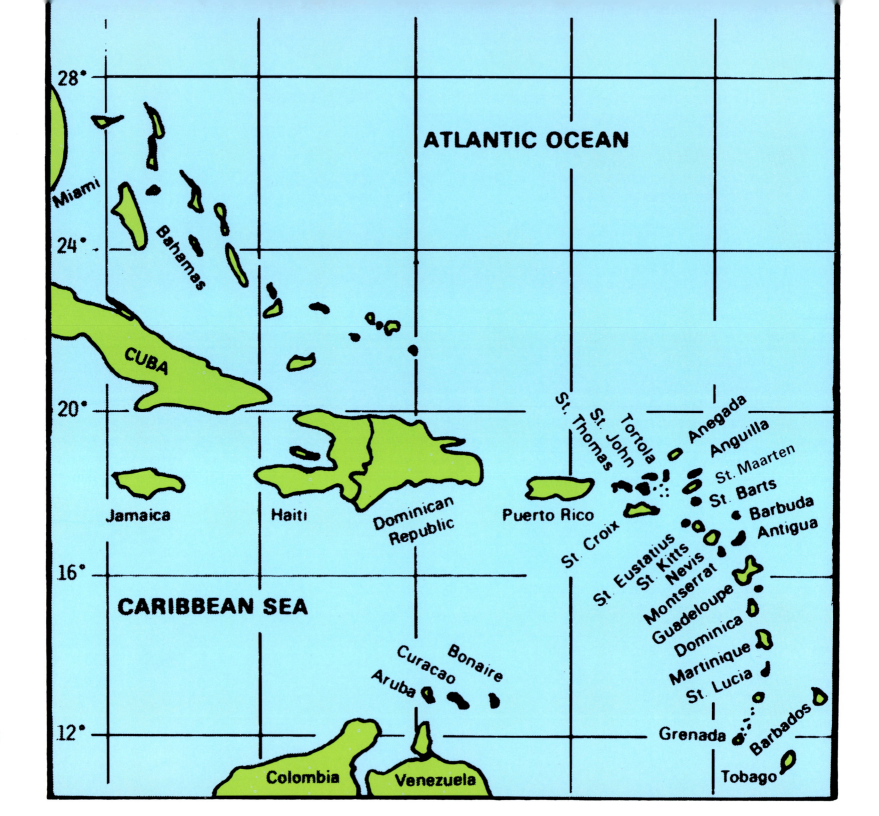

List of Plates

1. Early morning rainbow from the city of Les Trois-Ilets, Martinique taken from the seventh floor of Meridien Hotel.

2. Powerful water splashing on rocks–Antigua

3. Native Martinique fisherman mending his nets off the coast Sainte-Anne

4. One of the Caribbean's favorite sports–snorkeling. Magen's Beach, St. Thomas

5. View from the ferry approaching Fort-de-France, Martinique.

6. View from mountain top as rain storm begins to move in Tortola.

7. Windsurfer teaching his mate the art of windsurfing–Meridien Hotel, Martinique.

8. The crystal-clear, aqua blue waters and white sand beach–Orient Beach, St. Martin F.W.I.

9. One of the advantages of photographing in the Caribbean–we shoot, then we drink.

10. Sailors at the island of Tortola making a stop to stock their boat with supplies.

11. One of the major recreations in the Carribean is sailing–Tortola.

12. One of our favorite restaurants in the Caribbean is Antoine's, owned by Antoine and his wife located on Front Street–Philipsburg, St. Maarten, N.A.

13. Two of Antoine's specialties–Lobster Thermidor and Yellow Tail.

14. Roots on a tree–Guadeloupe.

15. Wild blueberries; fruit grows wild on the Volcanic Islands. One could never starve in the Caribbean–Dominica.

16. This unique hotel in St. Thomas is called Pavilions & Pools. Each room has its own spacious 20' x 14' completely private swimming pool surrounded by its own raised terrace and sunken garden.

17. The Holiday cruise ship in port at St. Maarten silhouetted with the moon.

18. One of the many delights of the Caribbean is the duty-free shopping–St. Thomas.

19. La Vie en Rose Restaurant on the French side of St. Martin and the Treasure Cove on the Dutch side of St. Maarten.

20. Old abandoned boat–St. Maarten.

21. Textures from buildings of locks and hinges.

22. & 23. The night lights of Charlotte Amalie, St. Thomas. Photographed from Bluebeard's Castle.

24. The town of Willemstad in Curacao, N.A., one of the major ports in the West Indies.

25. Horseback riding along the shore of the ocean. Another enjoyable pasttime in the Caribbean.

26. Fisherman inspecting his nets in Ocho Rios, Jamaica.

27. Fish for sale at Saturday morning market–St. Kitts.

28. Sunrise at Pineapple Beach, St. Thomas.

29. One of a hundred fresh water falls found in Jamaica.

30. & 31. Fresh peppers, squash, and avocados from open air market–St. Lucia.

32. Sunset over Philipsburg, St. Maarten, photographed from balcony of Holland House.

33. The romantic atmosphere of the Caribbean draws couples close together.

34. The Royal Princess cruise ship in port at Charlotte Amalie, St. Thomas.

35. Cruise ships Nordic Prince, Song of America and Festivale, in port at Charlotte Amalie, St. Thomas.

36. & 37. Episcopal and Methodist Churches in Philipsburg, St. Maarten

38. & 39. View of Coral World, Pineapple Beach and the Virgin Grand Hotel overlooking the island of St. John's in the distance (St. Thomas).

40. Windsurfer taken on the ferry from Fort-de-France to Les Trois-Ilets, Martinique.

41. The Orient Beach, St. Martin.

42. The largest hotel on the island of Martinique –the Meridien Hotel.

43. One of the beautiful flowers found throughout the Caribbean.

44. Café de Paris on the French side of St. Martin.

45. Sunset from the balcony of Bluebeard's Castle, St. Thomas.

46. The green, lush island of Tortola, which is still unspoiled by commercialism.

47. Martinique in October is the rainy season which makes it lush and green.

48. Mountain view of Magen's Beach, St. Thomas, is one of the ten finest beaches in the world.

49. Mullet Bay Resort, Dutch side, St. Maarten.

50. Reflections in the surf–Aruba.

51. Antoine's is a most romantic restaurant as it overlooks the ocean and one can hear the surf rolling in.

52. Homes on a hillside in Fort-de-France, Martinique.

53. One of the remaining forts, Fort de Marigot, St. Martin, used to protect their islands from their enemies in the beginnings of their history.

54. Texture as seen in the stones–St. Croix.

55. Homemade rum is made from sugar cane in this old rum factory–Tortola.

56. & 57. Overlooking the port of Charlotte Amalie, St. Thomas.

58. Animals roam free throughout the Caribbean.

59. Another beautiful flower found in the Caribbean.

60. For bad dog, refer to plate #61.

61. If you think this is bad, you should see what's under the water.

62. & 63. This represents our feelings of the islands–romantic!

64. & 65. Faces of the Caribbean.

66. Fishing village, Anse Dufour, Martinique.

67. Raging shore in San Juan, Puerto Rico.

68. & 69. Saturday morning market–St. Martin (French side).

70. Silhouette of fishing boats–St. Thomas.

2   3

16

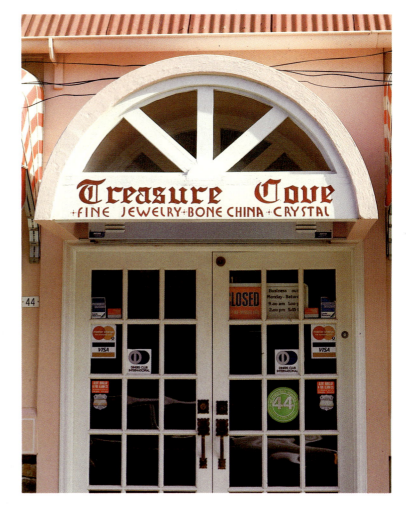

28

29

46

48

49

50

51

64